The Thing About Falling

Also by Tarriona "Tank" Ball

Vulnerable AF

The Thing About Falling

— POEMS —

Tarriona "Tank" Ball

The Thing About Falling in Love

The thing about falling is . . . it's never quite on purpose, is it? No one ever intends to trip or fall. So it kinda sounds like a mistake to me. I never planned to fall, and yet here I was stumbling into arms that I knew couldn't hold or catch me.

I love flying on a plane.
I have no choice but to sit and write. And like magic, there you are.

-Delta

Part I

The Feelings I Thought I Threw Away . . .

504

-Train

The moment I heard you were moving on
I felt like I was missing an empty train
The train had room for me
Could carry some of my bags
Maybe even make it to the destination
In time

But my train was leaving me
And I had my ticket in my hand and everything
And you were taking another passenger
To my destination

Her.
She.
Whatever.
Baggage claim bi.

But me
Waiting
Wondering
Woke up later and everything
Yet still I expected you to wait for me
Or even run after me

But I forgot
Trains never run after people . . .

They slug through the basements under the ground
Dragging behind all of our loaded suitcases

Going fast
Looking out for no one
Doors opening and closing
For whoever catches them in time

Alarms and bells ringing
Final boarding screaming
Tracks all mixed up
And here I am packing slowly

And so . . .
I missed it
Purposely

And yet
I was late.

And upset with you for leaving me at the station

Forgetting that trains wait for no one
Not even me.

When the news broke
So did I . . .
My breath went uneasy
Questions fell out of my mouth
And you looked at me like you didn't know I cared
I think we both did
I grew wings and feet that took me straight out of the door
I didn't know where I was going
But I couldn't stay where I was
Soon I returned to the scene of the crime
Face soaked
I held your hand because you probably would have held mine
I knew how scared you were in that moment because I knew how scared I was in that moment
You needed a friend
And I needed to be that friend
I knew this was a mistake that you couldn't take back
I knew that
I knew you were vulnerable and lonely
I knew she was shelter
I was once that too

-When the News Broke

"I hate this movie."

I didn't want front-row tickets to your new life.

-I Hate This Movie

It's been two years
And yet . . .
It's been a month

-Since We Broke Up

Sometimes it's a pause to feel nothing
Sometimes it's a pause to feel everything

-Standing on Business

We loved each other so much
And yet it still wasn't enough
So burnt in between and at the ends
Thoughts of her
Thoughts of him
Too often to count
Too real to count out
Your forever girl
I don't know what I was thinking . . .
Gifts to show my love
Sex to show my passion
Arguments to show my smarts
And yet I know I didn't give my all
But then again . . .
Why would I fall
For someone whose knees barely buckled for me

-Standing on Business . . . Or Not

Were you fucking her
This entire time?

-Sometimes I Wonder

-Intrusive Thoughts

Did you bend her over?
Did she moan loudly?
Fingers in her mouth?
Did you push deep?
Does she like it?
Eat her?
Suck you?
From the back?
Was it good?
Good enough to lie in?
Make a bed in?
Do you cum in anybody?
Build a future in any woman's body?
Who was she to you?
Special?
Can't be
But then again, what's special?
A new pair of jeans?
A shiny bracelet?
A car?
A new person to hide your new self in until your oldness
returns to its desk?
And your representatives' feet hurt . . .
Because even playing pretend gets exhausting, my love
Soon you will show up
And she'll see that all you are is who you've always been

GO TO SLEEP

-Keep Scrolling

When I put my phone down, I feel everything
And who wants that?

-Can't Let Go

We can't let go
Because we made plans
We wouldn't let go because we thought we had forever to get it right
Why would we let go? We put too many years in
We couldn't let go because we were betting on this one
We wouldn't let it loose because we looked back too many times
I didn't let go because no one else would love me
Or want me
Or hold me
Or need me
Or think of me in that special way that people think of people who are special . . .
We chose not to let go because it was still our choice to hold on
We didn't let go because
We simply didn't want to

A Letter to My Ex

What can be said that hasn't been already said? Haven't I been honest? Put all my cards on the table? I mean, at one point I really did think I was over it . . . until I wasn't.

What can I apologize for and mean it? I feel so different now. I think I can finally wish you well . . . far away from me now. I did love you and I think you loved me too, but I also believe it wasn't nearly enough on both sides, or not received the way we both actually see love.

FOR SALE
WAS HERE

There's a point when the toxicity feels normal
Feels familiar
Feels like home
And if we are home . . .
We might as well buy a couch
And since it's home . . .
We might as well get a table
And since it's home . . .
We should just buy the bed
Because we're clearly making ourselves
Very
Very comfortable
So we stayed
We stayed
Because we thought there was nowhere else for us to go . . .

-The Houses We Build

I thought
I wanted more
I'm not sure
If breaking up
Settled the score
Or opened the door
Now I'm even more upset than before
More confused than I was sure

-I Was Over It . . . Until I Wasn't

-Questions I Want to Ask Your Girlfriend

Does he still leave his shoes in the hallway?
Do you trip over them?
Does it bother you the way it bothered me?
Does he still leave the toothpaste with no cap?
Aggy, isn't it?
Does he still like his music loud, or does he consider you?
Wet gym clothes on the bed?
Spray too much cologne? Still use it like air freshener?
Does he still hate to hold hands in public? Does he still let go first?
Does it bother you
Like it bothered me?
Make you feel insecure . . .
Or unsure if he actually likes you?
Did you crawl inside?
Did you get quiet?
Distant?
Say it's nothing
When it was something
When it's always something . . .
Do you feel lonely next to him?
Was that just me?
Does he still tell you nothing is wrong when you ask him?
Does he still pretend there's no charger in sight when trying to reach him?
Is it still hard to reach him?
Is Netflix still a better boyfriend?
Yeah,
Thought so.

A Letter to My Ex

Better her than me.

Part II

The N Between Guy

It all started with this guy in my DM telling me I was pretty . . .

WELCOME

-No Alarm Detected . . .

Skinned knee
Bruised lip
And three Band-Aids later
You'd still fall again, wouldn't you?
Shoes untied
Silly String out
And doors unlocked . . .
Willing to let in anyone who turns the key

-Nu D

I lie in your arms
Naked
Vulnerable
And beautiful
Every part of me
Touched, kissed, and adored
Every compliment
A bouquet of my favorite flowers
Your lips
Sweet and soft
Tenderly touch mine
Every time
Your smile the best thing on your face
Butter knife smiles at me
Glimmer against cool metal
Your eyes yellow like the sun
I can't stare
Your lashes nice
Hands dark and long
The top so smooth and black
This feels like a warm bed

-I'm Okay with That

When the world becomes too loud and the static hurts my ears
I look for the shelter of your arms.
This dark creature finds me beautiful and desired and gives me a safe space to be woman and sexy and smart and hidden and seen and gentle and delicate and lovely all at the same time.
I like that space
I needed that space
My heart was rough
My attitude different
My ego bruised
My feelings fragile
And I needed someone to love me for the Tarriona I was.
In absolute silence
We connect in the dark
We share the desire to be felt and feel love
And tonight
I'm okay with that

A Letter to My Ex

Wait.

Hold up!

I know you not trying to switch up on me,
playboy!!!

-Da Fuk

I used to get a good-morning text
Good deep sex
A kiss on the neck before you head to work
A text to let me know you made it safe
A place to land
Softly
A person to call
Daily
FaceTimes just had me smiling
Couldn't wait to get off the stage to get on the phone
To tell you how my day was going
You had certain things that let me know I wanted these qualities
in my man
But I'm always so unsure
Always wanna play around some more before I lock the door
No wonder the brotha started getting restless

-I Clearly Like a Good Distraction

Relationships distract me
But I just gotta be held
Gotta yell
Gotta tell
Gotta tear
Down everything we built
And shared
I admit the fact that we failed
Hurt more than I'd like to tell
But
Shit happens
And we only remember a fraction
Of what really happened
While the rest is thrown in the trash
Discarded like it never happened

A Letter to My Ex

The toilet tissue was such a small ask.

Like really.

I hated that you thought you shouldn't do certain things for me because you felt like I was "good."

Because you felt like I was more financially stable. Because ima star . . .

How are we supposed to be anything or build anything if that's how you see me?

Like I'm undeserving of help.

These are honestly the things I have to remind myself of to be good on the situation, because though my body aches with the idea of no sex or being lonely when I don't want to be, I have to know that better will find me if I sit still and stop going back for seconds.

I really don't know how well that will sit with me, maybe I'm like my mom in that way . . . a way where, since I don't want to be alone, I'll put up with someone who doesn't want to be either.

-Sunset

I see you pulling away
Like a stray
Thought I was a ray
Of sunshine
But I guess we've had our good time
I guess you're done with the day . . .

-The Things We Forget . . .

You'll have to remember not feeling wanted
Or loved
Or cared about
Or valuable . . .
Just available
And ready
And wanting
And lonely
And waiting . . .
You'll have to remember that he chose rest over you
Or time alone
Or Wu-Tang
Or the game
Or the fight
You'll have to remember it's been two years with no movement
And how surprised you are that it's been two years

A Letter to My Ex

The loneliness is the greatest lesson. I really wanted to do better this time. I wanted to be a better communicator, more open and vulnerable about what I wanted and needed.

The crazy part is, I got a lot of what I wanted. The things I complained about were so small, but it doesn't mean they weren't important to me. Like dude . . . why couldn't you just ask if I wanted my nails done, or if I needed something for the house? Little things become so big in a small house, ya know.

HAPPY VALENTINES DAY!!
sorry
MAYBE NEXT YEAR
NH 4 TANK
LOVE

-Lonely Ass Valentine's

This year my Valentine's Day will be lonely
There will be no stuffed animals
There'll be no soft melted chocolates in my mouth
Or someone to suck the sweet stickiness off my tongue
There will be no balloons
No parade
No heart-shaped box
I've run someone else away . . .
I've gotten in the way of my own happiness again

A Letter to My Ex

Pussy straight aches. Titties hurt. Body wanna be grabbed, neck kissed, ass slapped . . . attention given. Lord, don't even talk about attention! But I need you to meet my standards. They're not impossible. So I ain't calling you tonight, playboy. Maybe in two days when my next loneliness kicks in. Maybe then.

-Why Don't You Bend for Me?

You really don't like me no more, huh?
If you did, you'd be trying to find your way into my arms
You'd be trying to love me
You would be throwing away the parts of yourself that I don't love
You're supposed to be bending yourself for me
Why aren't you aching for me the way I am for you?
Why aren't you hard yet?

I am so sorry for loving you so loud and so quiet all at the same time

-I Can See How That Would Have Been Confusing . . .

A Letter to My Ex

Maybe I should apologize. You really have always been your full self with me, and I'm the one who wanted you to want more for yourself and us. You were cool with the bare minimum, and on another planet that's cool . . . I'm sorry for acting like it actually was cool until it wasn't. I just wanted you to grow, forgetting completely that's not my decision.

A Letter to My Ex

I wanted to keep our friendship. I really did. But I know there is no space for you right now within what I'm trying to cultivate. I look back enough, honestly. And to be real, you had your chance. You had your time, and what did you do with it?

Part III

Something New . . .

I want plus-size happiness...

-Supersize Happiness

I want life-size happiness.
I want flowers just because it's Monday
I want soft kisses all over my face
The two for two
I want random love letters on my nightstand . . .
The strawberry shake
The heart-skip-a-beat Big Mac attack
The extra fries
The Happy Meal.
With the extra toy in it.
The sizzling-ass Sprite
I want good customer service
And I want it now

-Eve

The beginning is always so soft
So new
The texts
So quick
The calls
Never missed
The welcome mat on the outside of your heart
The folded sheets at the corners of your mouth
Every butterfly excited by its new wings
Each text a parade
Every FaceTime a love letter
Every encounter
A poem that you both write over and over

TANK
WELCOME
(The key is under the

-The Pink Elephant

It's too big to hide
Too loud to be kept quiet
Too beautiful not to share
Too funny not to laugh
Too high to come down
Too musical to not sound
You orchestrate the softness of me
You let me lie in the comfort of who God made me to be . . .
And that shit feels good.

-Permission

I'd like to have you.
You tell me I'm already yours.
I roll my eyes.
Can I really have you?
Can I have IT?
Am I allowed joy all over?
Love exhaled?
Black girl sureness?
The stuff my grandparents had?
The fifty-plus years of marriage?
The children?
A plant that grows?
A flower that continuously blooms?
Am I allowed . . .
Joy?

-Dear New Love

I choose you.

-Coloring Book

I notice colors more now, ya know
Paint
Drawings
Street art
Flowers
Children
Anything . . .
Beautiful little girls
Bouncing black boys
Haitian food
Warm weddings
People smiling
Pretty much anything that showers me with joy in the morning
Reminds me of you.

-Glowing

Recently
I've been told
That I glow
That I shine
That my night-light smile
Beams brighter
Than usual
And they can tell
It's you.

-Church

God.
You have made a believer out of me.

-White Easter Dress

Like red sno-ball-stained lips
Or fifty-cent frozen cups from Ms. Ella down the street
My love . . .
I melt for you
Drip for you
Ruin my Sunday best
Just
For you . . .

Dear New Lover,

I have never chosen love so purposefully.
I feel myself not falling in love but
walking in it with ballerina slippers
on. Just graceful, soft, intentional, and
beautiful. I'm choosing who I love
without letting my heart just run around
with no leash on, just falling and tripping
all over the place. Heart ain't have no
home training. My thirties needed that.

Dreaming

-Taking a Gazillion Pics

I hate the way my mind thinks of you
Makes me savor every moment
Stretch time
Takes a gazillion pictures
I wonder if I'm holding it too close
Holding us too tight
Too near
As if there's an alarm clock that will snap me out of my happiness
And if that's the case . . .
Why would I wake?

Sometimes
I'm afraid to hold on
Because I'm afraid to let go . . .

-Is That Love?

504

-Don't Forget to Remember

Remember when we met in Africa, my love?
Remember the way the orange sun shined on us and we fed the giraffes by the water in Lagos?
Remember how blue the water was?
We saw every fish.
Counted eight
The way you pierced the blue one with the spear
Made a fire and created us a feast for two
I don't like to eat fish, but I thought it was kinda special that you prepared it for me
I'll never forget the way the fire danced off your praline skin
Or the moon in your eyes
Or how you kept repeating
"This is amazing"
"This is amazing"
"This is amazing"
And it really was.
It really was.

-How We Talk

We talk to each other as if
We're trying to save our last relationship . . .
As if effective communication would have made everything better.
We talk to each other like: "See, it wasn't me!"
Like: "Look at what I do with a good person.
I do right by them.
Let me show you."

-Loving a Black Man in America

Make it back home to me, please.
Because when I say "be safe"
I mean be smart
I mean be conscious
I mean treat yourself like you're precious
Like glass
Like cargo that somebody paid $49.99 plus extra n shipping
To make sure that you make it just in time
Can you drive more safely?
Please, can you stop treating your wheels like wind?
Like you come and go as you please?
As if no one is waiting on you
As if I haven't been waiting for you . . .

Dear New Love,

Even while dating others, I've always looked around the corner to see who could be better for me. A better fit. Get along better with my friends. Kiss my mama on the cheek, love me deeper. Pray for me. Be my friend. Look out for "ya girl." That's you.

I'm ready to get on the roller coaster even though the last one just scared the shit out of me. But even with the last one, I knew it was preparing me for the ride of a lifetime. Teaching me how to speak, approach, date, love, and communicate with someone intimately. I've done it so wrong I have no choice but to approach it differently this time. And I feel so lucky to do it with someone who I really feel accepts all my parts as I learn to accept his.

Ya know, Stevie Wonder always plays when you're near; it reminds me that my daddy is watching us from heaven, and guess what . . . we're the best movie he's seen in years.

HILLMAN

LOVE
IT'S THE
NOLA WAY

Acknowledgments

I'd like to acknowledge my publisher and close friends for helping me to complete this book. I'd even like to strangely thank myself for being vulnerable AF and honest with myself about what I was going through so others would know that they are not alone. People should know that I too had to put myself back together again, and again, and again.

About the Author

Tarriona "Tank" Ball is a New Orleans–based poet and Grammy-winning recording artist with her band, Tank and the Bangas. This is her second book of poetry.

Follow Tank

instagram.com/thinktank20
tankandthebangas.com
youtube.com/TankandtheBangas
instagram.com/tankandthebangas
x.com/tankanddabangas
faccbook.com/TankAndTheBangas

Enjoy *The Thing About Falling* as an audiobook narrated by the author, wherever books are sold.

The authorised representative in the EEA is Simon and Schuster Netherlands BV, Herculesplein 96 3584 AA Utrecht, Netherlands. (info@simonandschuster.nl)

Andrews McMeel Publishing
a division of Andrews McMeel Universal
1130 Walnut Street, Kansas City, Missouri 64106

www.andrewsmcmeel.com

25 26 27 28 29 TEN 10 9 8 7 6 5 4 3 2 1

ISBN: 979-8-8816-0021-1

Library of Congress Control Number: 2024950928

Illustrations by Shonté Young-Williams